Timmy Mallett's Utterly Brilliant History of the World

Pictures by Ashley Haynes

Official Historian Aisling O'Hagan

... Castle Mallett was under attack !!
Prince Timmy was desperate !

Fixing his secret Mallett to the flag pole
he gasped as the sun shone on it
revealing brave ancient heroes leaping
to his rescue.

Do like Prince Timmy, hold the
horrorgram to a bright light
to see something utterly, horribly
brilliant ...

so there !

TIMMY MALLETT'S UTTERLY BRILLIANT HISTORY OF THE WORLD was first
published in Piccolo in 1991 by Pan Books Ltd., Cavaye Place, London SW10 9PG

Text © Timmy Mallett 1991
Illustrations © Ashley Haynes 1991
All rights reserved

ISBN 0 330 30795 9

Printed in England by Clays Ltd, St Ives plc

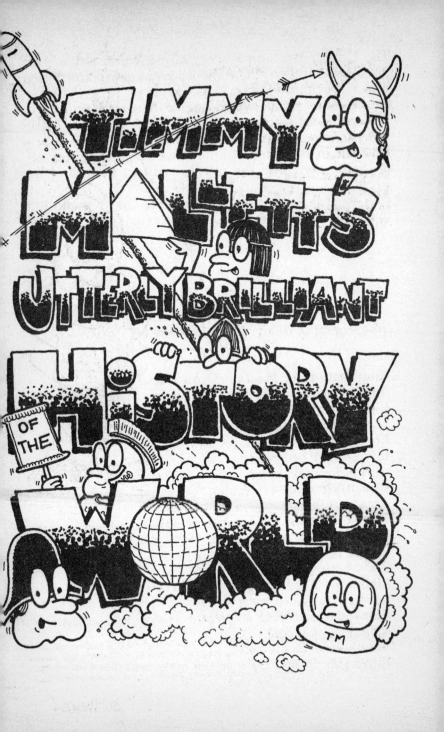

TIMMY MALLETT'S UTTERLY BRILLIANT HISTORY OF THE WORLD

The Utterly Brilliant History of the World is the most fascinating subject the world has ever known. The reason it is so fascinating is because I wrote it!

So, before I begin, I would like to thank certain utterly brilliant people for making this book possible: firstly myself, for writing it, secondly myself, for being utterly brilliant in this area of knowledge and thirdly myself, for being born into the utterly brilliant history of the world.

And so, it is with utter thanks to me that I would like to dedicate this book to ... myself!

Not forgetting utterly special thanks to:

King Arthur, *for lending me his round table.*
Julius Caesar, *for lending me his ears.*
King William, *for lending me his orange.*
Marie Antoinette, *for letting me eat her cake.*
Mary Queen of Spots, *for lending me her head.*
Edward, *for confessing.*
Alfred, *for more cakes.*
Queen Victoria, *for keeping me amused.*
Excalibur, *for getting to the point.*
The Bolsheviks, *for being so bolshy.*
Francis Drake, *for the game of bowls.*
Elizabeth, *for being the first.*
Gladstone, *for his bag.*
Cleopatra, *for walking like an Egyptian.*
Achilles, *for being such a heel.*
Alexander, *for being so great.*
Marco, *for his polo.*
Beethoven, *for his notes.*
Alexander Graham, *for giving me a bell.*
Ivan, *for being so terrible.*

CHAPTER ONE:
NOTHING

A lot of people believe that before the utterly brilliant history of the world began — in other words in the beginning — there was nothing. This is not true. There was never nothing. How do I know there was never nothing? Simple, I found out. What did I find out? NOTHING!

EVERYDAY LIFE BEFORE THE WORLD BEGAN

Many people who lived in the time of nothing have told me that although they enjoyed doing nothing, life did get rather boring. There was nothing on the television, nothing to read, nothing to see and nothing to talk about. Not only that – when they complained about nothing they were told they had nothing to complain about! Although we know nothing about this period of history, many things have survived that tell us about nothing.

FASHION IN THE TIME OF NOTHING

During this period in history, people wore nothing.

BOOKS IN THE TIME OF NOTHING

Much Ado about Nothing by William Shakespeare
Making something out of Nothing, by No One In Particular
Learn about Nothing, by No One You'd Remember

A POEM ABOUT NOTHING

Tum ti ta tar ti tum
Bum ti la tum ti ti
La la la ti tum ti ti
Tum ta ta tum ti li.

WHERE TO GO TO SEE NOTHING

A dark room
A blank page
Space
Your brain

GREAT THINGS YOU CAN DO WITH NOTHING

1. Stare out of your window at it
2. Say you're thinking about it
3. Earn it
4. Eat it
5. Take it to school and say it's your homework
6. Fill your head with it

FOOTNOTE.....
MEANWHILE... IN THE REST
OF THE WORLD... NOTHING
WAS HAPPENING!!.....

A QUIZ ABOUT NOTHING

One of the two pictures below is of nothing. Can you guess which one?

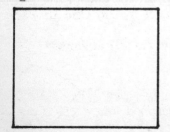

If you would like to re-enact what life was like in these times – spend the day doing nothing!

CHAPTER TWO:
THE BEGINNING OF THE WORLD

After squillions and squillions of years of loads of nothing, all of a sudden, one afternoon, there was a big bang, and the universe came together and the world began. Fortunately nothing in particular was going on at the time although many people did complain of a headache afterwards.

In fact many people were not at all happy about the world beginning, seeing as how, after the big bang had banged, there was a considerable amount of tidying up to do and some found themselves living in a completely different country from the one they had started off in. Still – at least they now had something to complain about!

A QUICK QUIZ ABOUT THE BIG BANG

1. Which of the following sounds is closest to the noise made by the big bang? (You may use your brain to answer this question)
   a) Bang!
   b) Ba. . . . ng! !
   c) . . . . ngggg! ! !
   d) Puffffffffffffffff . . . . . . t!

2. Out of the four pictures below, which do you think looks most like the big bang? (you may look at the pictures to answer this question)

THINGS TO DO. . .

▼

1. Make a big bang
2. Have some bangers for tea
3. Bang your head on the table

CHAPTER THREE:

PREHISTORY

A short time after the big bang and a while before the world got into full swing, came a period in history known as Prehistory, which came around the year 000.000.000.000.1000, BC.

FOSSILS

Fossilized pimple

Fossilized piece of chewing gum

Fossilized school report

Fossils are the things left over from prehistoric times that, over squillions and squillions of years, have turned into stone. By studying them we can build up a picture of what life was like in these times. A person who studies fossil remains is called a brainyologist!

PLANT LIFE

Many plants did not have a happy life during prehistoric times.

I'M SO SAD I THINK I'M GOING TO POT!

MOVING CONTINENTS

Many continents decided to move house during prehistoric times.

BRRRR!....I'M FED UP OF BEING COLD... I'M MOVING SOUTH TO A WARM CLIMATE!......

ROCK

The oldest thing on earth is rock, which was first formed over one thousand squillion years ago. Unfortunately most of the earth's rock got eaten during prehistoric times. Someone who eats the earth's rocks is called – greedy!

SEA LIFE

The very first fish to arrive on the earth were called Fish Fingers. They had no head, no arms, no legs and they could not swim. What is unusual about them is that they were covered in a strange substance known as bread-crumbs. They also got eaten for tea!

THINGS TO DO
▼

1. Go and fossilize your pimples.
2. Pretend you are a fossil and don't get out of bed for a week!

CHAPTER FOUR:
DINOSAURS, MAMMALS AND THE BIRTH OF MAN

A great many people believe that squillions and squillions of years ago dinosaurs ruled the earth. This has been proved true by the discovery of an ancient polaroid snap shown below. Life for the average dinosaur was heavy going and eventually they died out, although some went on to become famous film stars.

FAMOUS DINOSAUR RULERS

Timmy saurus rex I
Bronte Monty the great
Roget's Thesaurus, who ate his own words
Run out of Breathasaurus the unfit

ANCIENT LAWS PASSED BY DINOSAURS

1. Ask before you eat people
2. Offer your seat to bigger dinosaurs or those with heavy shopping
3. Put someone's hand in your mouth when you cough!

DINOSAUR FASHION

Although most dinosaurs were extremely ugly, they were also extremely fashion conscious. The typical dinosaur liked to wear green and often favoured large baggy clothes that disguised their fuller figure. Polo necks were also popular as they fitted comfortably over most trunks and in summer the trendy dinosaur would sport a natty pair of cycling shorts that were casual but suitable to wear when eating bicycles.

MAMMALS

Mammals are exactly the same as camels, but spelt differently. Look them up in a natural history book under P.

DINOSAUR JOKE

Q. What do you call a one-eyed dinosaur?
A. *D'yathinkeesaurus!*

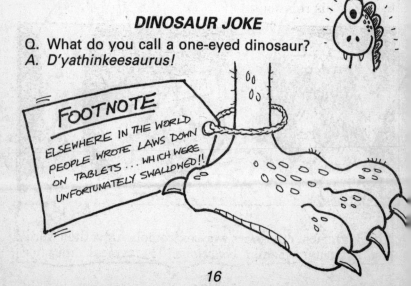

FOOTNOTE

ELSEWHERE IN THE WORLD PEOPLE WROTE LAWS DOWN ON TABLETS ... WHICH WERE UNFORTUNATELY SWALLOWED!!

THE BIRTH OF MAN

Many people believe that men evolved from the ape. Can you guess where women came from?

MAN'S RELATIVES

According to legend, man is related to a group of animals called primates. Here is an ancient letter written by man to one of his relations:

CLUES FROM TEETH

Many fossil jaws have been found that tell us much about the life of early man.

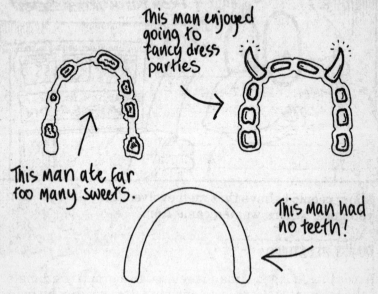

This man enjoyed going to fancy dress parties

This man ate far too many sweets.

This man had no teeth!

FOSSIL SKULLS

These two skulls belong to early man. The one on the right has a pea-sized brain. Can you guess which one was more stupid?

THINGS TO DO
▼

1. Become an ape
2. Measure the size of your brain

CHAPTER FIVE:
THE DAFT AGES

After the birth of man, came three ages. The Stone Age,
The Iron Age and The Bronze Age.

THE STONE AGE

The Stone Age people are most famous for living in the Stone Age. Unfortunately they were unable to invent much because they wore stone clothes, and were unable to get about much. Because of this they were always stony broke and eventually became stone deaf because no one would talk to them. Perhaps one of the most famous stone remains remaining from the Stone Age is Stone Henge, a collection of rather big stones.

People who lived in the Iron Age are most famous for inventing the iron. Because of this they spent most of their days ironing, which was difficult as most of their clothes were still made of stone.

Iron age people LOVED heavy metal music! Iron Mallett, Def Mallett, Bon Timmy etc. They were obviously still STONE deaf!

THE BRONZE AGE

People alive during the Bronze Age are most famous for coming third – which is probably why they came after the stone and iron age. They did, however, manage to collect a large number of bronze medals which they then, rather cleverly, melted down to make more bronze medals.

SONG SUNG BY EARLY MAN

Early man enjoyed singing. This song tells us much about prehistoric life.

Grunt grunt gerrrunt, grunt grunt gerrrrunt
Grunt grunt geruuuuuunt . . . . . . grunt, grunt, grunt.

Can you guess what it's about?   (Try watching the video!)

CONCLUSION

Although life was hard for people who lived in these ages it is their own fault for not being born later.

THINGS TO DO

▼

1. Your ironing
2. Make a tasty cake out of the following ingredients:-
   Stone, Iron and Bronze

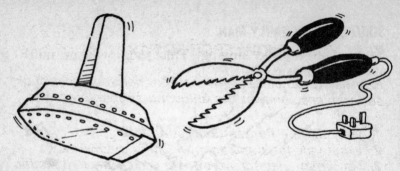

The picture above shows an Iron Age thing made out of iron, which may have been used for ironing. It was found in my pocket where other objects were also found.

An ancient electric razor. These were very handy due to the fact that early man was extremely hairy!

Early man made jewellery from animal teeth, bones and tusks. Here's how to make yours.

HOW TO MAKE A MAMMOTH TOOTH NECKLACE

WHAT YOU WILL NEED:

One dead mammoth, string

WHAT TO DO:

1. Pluck out the teeth from your dead mammoth
2. Wash them
3. Drill a hole through them
4. Thread them on your string
5. Put them back again

TEST YOUR KNOWLEDGE SO FAR

In order to be certain you have understood this book so far, please answer the following simple questions:

1. Why did the Roman Civilization fall?
2. What was the population of China in 2500 BC?
3. How many letters were there in the ancient Arabic alphabet?

If you cannot answer more than four of the above questions then I suggest you go back to the beginning and start again, this time paying a great deal more attention. Off you go.

TEST YOUR EYESIGHT SO FAR

Spot the dinosaur in this picture

If you cannot spot the dinosaur in this picture – go and get your eyes tested. Off you go!

CHAPTER SIX:
THE EGYPTIANS

Unlike the Romans or the Greeks, the Egyptians were Egyptian and came from Egypt around the time of 86 years BC. In other words, yonks ago. The Egyptians were quite a cheeky lot and were always being told off for painting on walls and locking their mummies in dark cupboards when they couldn't get their own way. Apart from this the Egyptians learnt the ancient craft of spinning, which of course made them extremely dizzy and explains why their houses were all shaped like upside down funnels.

TUTANKHAMUN

Tutankhamun, or Tut for short, was made King of Egypt when he was still a young boy. All was going well until one day Tut was wrapped in a giant bandage and shoved inside a tomb. Unfortunately the tomb was not opened again until 1922 by which time Tut was fairly annoyed, and not in the mood for socializing.

HOW TO WALK LIKE AN EGYPTIAN

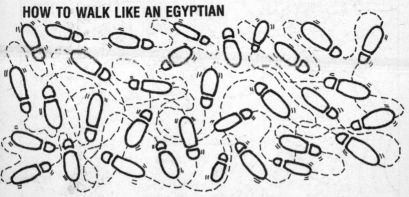

To walk like an Egyptian simply walk normally but place one hand in front of your face and the other behind your bottom. (See picture.) Do not forget to move.

TUT'S TOMB

Ancient Egyptians practised the custom of placing sacred items inside the tomb for their kings to take with them after they died. In this picture are ten things Tut chose to take with him. See if you can find them:–

1. *Sony Walkman*
2. *Sandwiches*
3. *Pack of cards*
4. *Skateboard*
5. *False nose*
6. *Wendy hut*
7. *Bicycle*
8. *Chess set*
9. *Pet dog*
10. *Alarm clock*

ANCIENT LETTER FOUND IN TUT'S TOMB...

LET ME OUT

TUTANKHAMUN JOKE

What did King Tut say to the bloke who discovered his tomb?
Toot and come in!

Egyptians wore Egyptian wigs hired from fancy dress shops.

A pharoah's hat - possibly made from old football socks.

HOW TO MAKE YOUR OWN PYRAMID

For this you will need:

A large pair of scissors
Your house

WHAT TO DO:

Cut off the bottom of your house so that only the roof remains. (See diagram.)

CLEOPATRA

Cleopatra was the ruler of Egypt round about 51 BC to 30 BC. Although she was quite fashionable, starred in many films and won countless fancy-dress competitions, she is probably most famous for her knitting. In 1900 Cleopatra was presented with a giant stone needle by Embankment Station in London, but, as it was made of stone and weighed a squillion tons, she was unfortunately unable to lift it and so left it where it was, where it remains to this day. What a Knit!

PLACES TO VISIT

1. Egypt

THINGS TO DO

1. Wrap up your mummy
2. Have a bath with the milkman

CHAPTER SEVEN:
THE GREEKS

Greek civilization began a great deal of years ago in Greece, a country famous for its unfurnished buildings, otherwise known as ruins. To this day the Greeks are most famous for inventing vases, olives, goats, the Olympic games and kebabs, named after the well known Greek chef, Donna Kebab. The Greeks are also fairly famous for inventing thinking, which they put a great deal of thought into – I think!

EVERYDAY LIFE IN ANCIENT GREECE

Houses and palaces were decorated with frescos like these. A fresco is a picture painted on the plaster of a wall while the plaster is still damp.

HOW TO MAKE A GREEK FRESCO IN YOUR LIVING ROOM

What you will need:–

- *Concrete (works better than plaster)*
- *A wall (indoors if it's raining)*
- *Your bath (to mix the concrete in)*
- *Loads of paint.*

The skill in fresco painting is to get it done while your parents are out – to surprise them.

To make your fresco, put on your best clothes, mix a ton of concrete in your bath, scoop up as much as you can in your arms. Carry it downstairs, slap it on your chosen wall and while it is still dripping chuck on as much paint as possible.

THE OLYMPIC GAMES

Every four years from 776 BC the Greeks held a great festival for athletes in honour of the great Greek god Zeusless the Useless at Sports. These were held at Olympia and thus became known as the Olympic Games.

ANCIENT GREEK SPORTS PLAYED AT THE FIRST OLYMPIC GAMES

- Urn and spoon race
- Spot the olive in the field
- Throw the wellie at the ruin
- Pin the carrot on the donkey
- Pass the god.

THINGS TO DO

▼

1. Go and sit in a large tub of lard. By doing this you can imagine what life was like in Greece. (Get it? !)
2. Design a roof for the Acropolis and then ruin it.
3. Practise the ancient urn and spoon race using a priceless vase and a teaspoon.

FAMOUS GREEKIE PEOPLE

1. George Michael
2. Zeus

LARGE GREEK JARS

Large Greek jars such as these were called large Greek jars

ANCIENT GREEK JOKE

Q. How much does a Greek Urn?
A. *About fifty quid!*

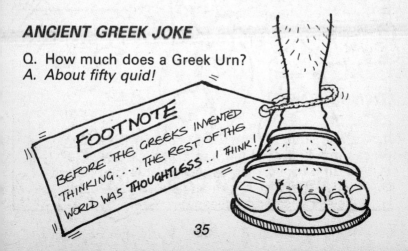

CHAPTER EIGHT:
THE CHINESE EMPIRE

Civilization in China began yonks and yonks and yonks ago and the majority of its dense population evolved from vases around the year 1500 BC. Life for the ancient chinese vase was bitterly hard and, as a result, many had chips on their shoulders.

Despite being a vase, ancient Chinese man was able to advance by sticking his 'wok' on the front of his house enabling him to pick up educational TV programmes such as 'WOKADAY'. He also became expert at playing chopsticks on the piano, which annoyed neighbouring countries.

HOW TO MAKE A CHINESE HAT

- Take a lampshade, being careful not to soil it with dirty fingerprints.
- Cut out all the lumpy bits from inside
- Punch out two holes for elastic
- Put it on your head
- Go and show your mum.

FAMOUS CHINESE PEOPLE

Ping Pong
Sing Song
King Kong

ANCIENT CHINESE WRITING

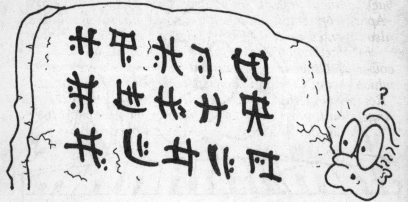

Unfortunately we are unable to read this valuable stone as it was written before writing was invented.

THINGS TO DO

▼

● Dress up as a Chinese vase
● See if your Mum's best china is real by throwing it out of your bedroom window, frisby-style
● Collect up all the bits and build the Great Wall of China!

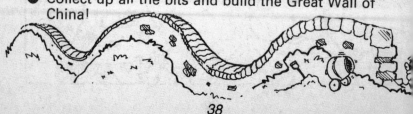

CHAPTER NINE:
THE MIGHTY ROMAN EMPIRE

After China and Greece, the next great civilization was that of ancient Rome. The history of ancient Rome dates back to about 750 BC and started in a place called Italy. Apart from being famous for conquering, the Romans also invented central heating. Hence chief radiator fitter became known as Gladiator, and was all hot and powerful. Other things invented by Romans were: roads, which meant they had somewhere to park their chariots, Roman numerals, which meant they could count their fingers and more importantly, money, which meant they could finally use phone boxes and phone home.

ROMAN PASTIMES

At weekends many Roman generals were invited to Toga parties which they attended wearing their bed sheet with a hole cut in the middle.

ROMAN POETRY

A few priceless works by poets and authors have survived in libraries. These tell us a little bit about life in Roman times.

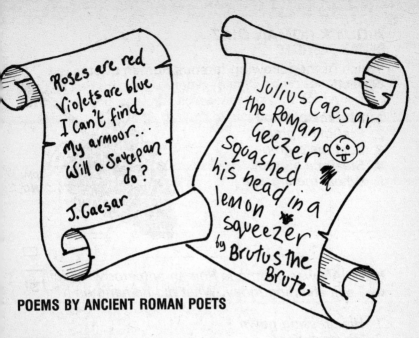

Roses are red
Violets are blue
I can't find
My armour...
Will a Saucepan
do?

J. Caesar

Julius Caesar
the Roman
Geezer
Squashed
his head in a
lemon
squeezer
by Brutus the
Brute

POEMS BY ANCIENT ROMAN POETS

ROMAN BATHS

After a hard day at the battle, Roman men relaxed in what were called Roman Baths, which were decorated with marble and gold.

HOW TO MAKE A ROMAN BATH

Tell him he pongs
Take his clothes off
Chuck him in the tub.

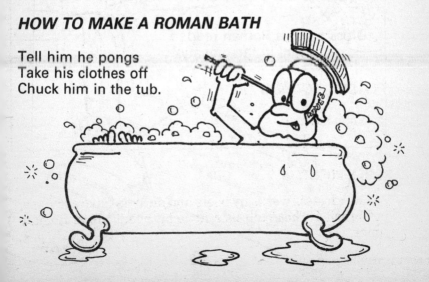

A QUICK ROMAN QUIZ

Which of the following famous Roman quotes is correct:–

1. Peel me a grape
2. Feel me a grape
3. Deal me a grape
4. Steal me a grape
5. Wheel me a grape

HADRIAN was a famous Roman emperor who built a wall still standing today. What did he hang on it?

1. His dressing gown
2. His dartboard
3. A poster of his favourite football team
4. Some handy shelves

THINGS TO DO

1. Dress up as a Roman road
2. Go a-roamin' in the gloamin'

PLACES TO VISIT

1. Your bath.

FOOTNOTE

ONCE THE ROMANS HAD INVENTED COUNTING, MANY PEOPLE IN THE WORLD FOUND OUT THEY WERE A LOT OLDER THAN THEY THOUGHT!!....

CHAPTER TEN:
THE END OF THE ROMAN EMPIRE

Roman soldiers started to leave Britain in about 400 AD when, thankfully, they had had enough baths and built enough roads to clear off out of it.

What followed was a period lasting a long time when people of Europe spent their days cleaning out baths, repairing holes in bedsheets rescued from toga parties, paying off the central-heating bills, picking up grape pips, rearranging the sofas again and chucking naff ornamental lumps of pottery at rude and unfashionably dressed barbarian invaders with daft names such as Huns, Goths, Visigoths, extremely Visigoths, and Vandals!

Unfortunately the Romans rather selfishly took their candles with them and, seeing as how no one had invented electricity yet, Britain was thrown into a rather bitterly hard period known as **the Dark Ages**.

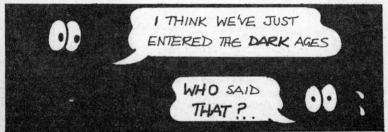

LIFE IN THE DARK AGES...

DARK AGES JOKE

Q. How long did the Dark Ages last?
A. Ages and ages!

FOOTNOTE

BARBARIAN INVADERS, WHO INVADED
FRANCE, WERE KNOWN AS FRANKS!..
.. ONCE DEFEATED, THEY WERE MELTED
DOWN AND MADE INTO CANS !!...

DIG IT!

Archaeology is all about piecing together the ancient things that people left behind, to gain a picture of how they lived. The word 'Archaeology' comes from ancient times and when translated means 'nosey old swot'.

WHAT YOU WILL NEED TO BE AN ARCHAEOLOGIST

- **A big nose**
- **Plenty of glue** – to mend all the broken pieces
- **Coloured pencils** – to finish off all those cave drawings
- **A bunch of flowers** – to stick in ancient vases
- **A duster** – some temples and tombs get very dusty
- **A mechanical digger** – to get the job done quicker
- **An ancient newspaper** – to check what's on TV
- **Sandwiches** – ancient food can make you feel a bit ill
- **A hoover** – metal detectors are not allowed in some ruins
- **A phone** – many ancient buildings do not have one

WHAT TO DO IF YOU FIND SOMETHING

Many young people have made important discoveries. If you find evidence of ancient times that you think is extremely valuable you will need to take the following steps:—

1. Don't tell anyone
2. If it's a coin, try it in the nearest chocolate machine
3. If it's a bone, give it to the dog
4. If it's valuable, sell it to your parents for Christmas.

THINGS YOU CAN DO

A useful way to learn about archaeology is to take a notebook on all your expeditions and use the pages to make paper aeroplanes.

HOW CAN WE TELL HOW OLD SOMETHING IS?

● Place the object on the ground and stamp on it. If it crumbles, it is extremely ancient and valuable
● Look for a date on it. If there isn't one, carve your own.

HOW TO DO YOUR OWN DIG

Archaeologists often have to dig into the ground to uncover ancient things. This is called a 'dig', and the place where the dig takes place is called a 'site'.

HOW TO PLAN AND ORGANIZE YOUR DIG

1. Choose your site. If your mum is always telling you 'your room is a site', then this is a good place to start.

2. Using a bucket and spade, dig up your entire bedroom, being careful not to destroy anything in the process.

3. When you have dug up your room remember to take a photograph. This is a useful way of using up old film!

KEEPING RECORDS

Keeping records will help future archaeologists work out the value of their own finds. Kylie Minogue albums are, however, an exception.

PIECING THE EVIDENCE TOGETHER

As a trained archaeologist I have picked out various objects found in my own bedroom dig that have now become priceless evidence of our past.

DIRTY OLD SOCK This dirty old sock, found underneath my floorboards, shows that ancient people only wore one sock.

MOULDY CUP OF TEA Tea originally originated in China yonks ago. Evidence from this old cup reveals that the person who drank from it did not wash it up.

TOYS AND GAMES This flattened football reveals that ancient people played with a flat football.

HALF-FINISHED HOMEWORK This piece of half-finished homework found stuffed between my wardrobe and the wall shows us that even in ancient times people stuffed their half-finished homework down the side of their wardrobe.

BOOKS TO READ

1. *How to Rebuild your Bedroom* by I. M. Sorrymum
2. *How to Get Your Ancient Mummy Out From Under Your Floorboards* by O. Dear.

CHAPTER ELEVEN:
THE VIKINGS

After the Dark Ages, Britain was invaded by invaders known as Saxons, Normans and Vikings. As I remember, it was no picnic living here at this time, due to the fact that no one knew who was going to come knocking on their front door next.

THE VIKINGS

The word 'Viking' means 'Why do you want to be king here when you can be king everywhere?' (It was said with a Norwegian accent and thus became shortened to Vi-king.)

The Vikings came to Britain from Norway, Sweden and Denmark around the time of AD 789 when, unfortunately for us, they got bored with sitting around in pine saunas all day, listening to A-Ha records and annoying goats, and decided to go on holiday to annoy someone else.

Although the Vikings spent most of their holiday bashing people on the head, looting villages, setting fire to things, making fun of the animals and generally carrying on in a rather rude way, they were, on the whole, not such a bad crowd and many of their inventions, such as eating and writing poems, have remained with us today.

VIKING POEM

Many Vikings wrote poems called sagas, which told stories of their brave gods. Here is a typical saga recited after a hearty feast:

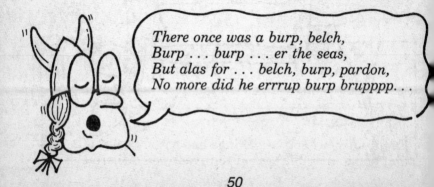

There once was a burp, belch,
Burp . . . burp . . . er the seas,
But alas for . . . belch, burp, pardon,
No more did he errrup burp brupppp . . .

TYPICAL VIKING SNACK

The Vikings loved feasting. They ate large quantities of food, and anything else that was lying around, which was then washed down with vast quantities of anything else that was lying around. Here is what became known as a 'Vikisnack', probably eaten around 11 am, between breakfast and brunch.

Starters

Horse legs, tree stumps or hedge soup

Main Course

A large house topped with one or two roads

Vegetables of the day

Oak tree, fence or chipped longboats.

Pud

Mountain peaks with helmet-horn custard

Eventually, when the Vikings had eaten us out of house and home, they burped off to invade somewhere else.

THINGS TO DO

▼

1. Make a Viking ship out of your bed
2. Eat a typical Viking meal without moving your lips.

DAYS OF THE WEEK

The Vikings also invented seven of our days of the week. Can you guess which ones?

1. *Yesterday*
2. *Holiday*
3. *Off day*
4. *Birthday*
5. *Wacaday*
6. *Mother's Day*
7. *Not today, thank you*

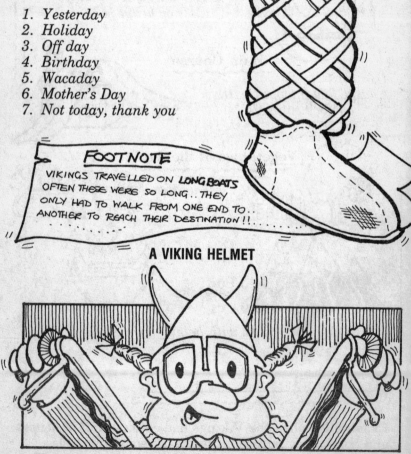

FOOTNOTE

VIKINGS TRAVELLED ON LONGBOATS OFTEN THESE WERE SO LONG.. THEY ONLY HAD TO WALK FROM ONE END TO.. ANOTHER TO REACH THEIR DESTINATION!!...

A VIKING HELMET

These were worn at all times when riding motorbikes.

CHAPTER TWELVE:
THE SAXONS AND THE NORMANS

Sometime around AD, 383 British big chiefs invited the Anglo-Saxons, who were at that time on holiday in Germany, to help them chase off Barbarian tribes that were beginning to get on everyone's nerves. The only problem was, once they had finally got here and settled in, they didn't really feel like going back. Not only that, they went and invited all their friends over as well. What followed was a jolly long scrap which was won by the Anglos who then took over the whole country until Norman conquested in 1066.

The word 'Anglo-Saxon' means 'I'm staying here, tough luck'.

FRIEND OR FOE?....

TOURISTS!!!

HI... I'M NORMAN THE NORMAN!

ANGLO SAXON

SAXON ANGLE

90°

ANGLO-SAXON AND NORMAN KINGS

KING ARTHUR

According to legend, the Anglo-Saxons were led by a great king named Arthur. The only snag was, for some strange reason, King Arthur wouldn't step out of the house without taking an enormous round table with him, which was a bit of a drag.

ARTHUR'S TABLE

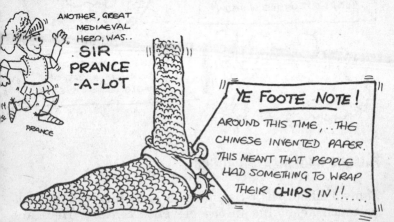

ANGLO-SAXON TREASURES

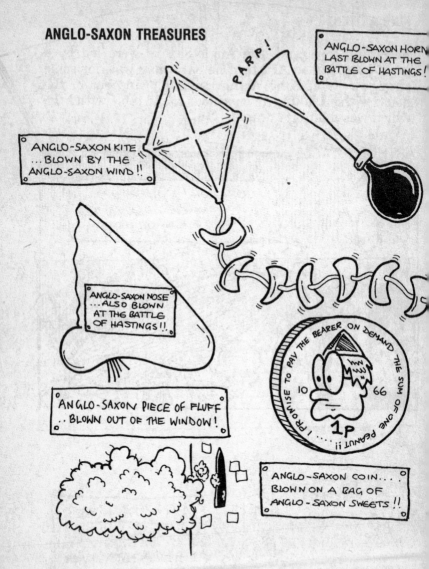

PARP!

ANGLO-SAXON HORN LAST BLOWN AT THE BATTLE OF HASTINGS!

ANGLO-SAXON KITE ...BLOWN BY THE ANGLO-SAXON WIND!!

ANGLO-SAXON NOSE ...ALSO BLOWN AT THE BATTLE OF HASTINGS!!

ANGLO-SAXON PIECE OF FLUFF ..BLOWN OUT OF THE WINDOW!

I PROMISE TO PAY THE BEARER ON DEMAND THE SUM OF ONE PEANUT!!
10
66
1P

ANGLO-SAXON COIN.... BLOWN ON A BAG OF ANGLO-SAXON SWEETS!!

FAMOUS ANGLO-SAXON BOOKS

Many ancient Anglo-Saxon books have survived that tell us much about life in the eleventh century. Here are some of them:–

QUIZ

Q. Many strange objects were found buried in Anglo-Saxon grounds. What do you think this is?

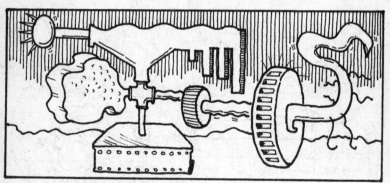

A. I haven't the foggiest!

THE BATTLE OF HASTINGS

The Battle of Hastings, fought between William and Harold, is probably the most famous battle of all time. It began at nine o'clock in the morning on 14 October 1066, and finished at five o'clock that afternoon, when the majority of Saxons had to leave to catch the last bus home. Although cameras were not allowed in, fortunately a teacloth-maker happened to be passing by and recorded the legendary battle for ever. He called his teacloth the Bayeux Tapestry.

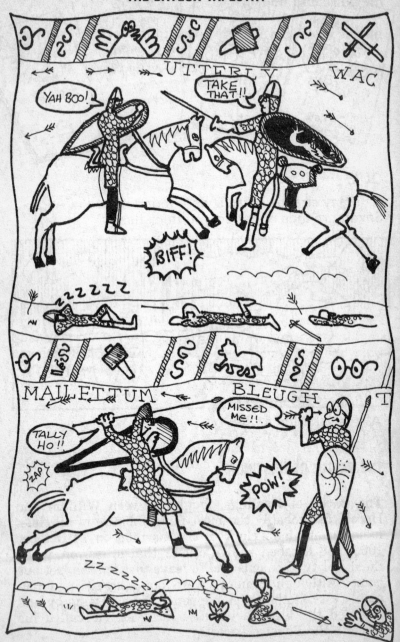

THE DOMESDAY BOOK

Just as we all have favourite bedtime books and stories, so William the Conker did too. His was called the Domesday Book.

The Domesday Book contained information about every single person in the country. What their mum and dad did, what they ate for dinner, what their favourite colour was and what they wanted to do when they grew up. Here are some of the questions that William asked in his famous Domesday Book:

1. *How do you spell 'Cat'?*
2. *Would I look better with my hair short?*
3. *Was I a bit nasty to Harold?*

THINGS TO DO

- Make a fashionable William the Conker outfit out of a teacloth.
- Go to Hastings and look for Harold's eye.
- Find out the name of every single person in the country.

CHAPTER THIRTEEN:
THE MIDDLE AGES

Once the Normans had successfully succeeded at the Battle of Hastings they proceeded to spend the rest of their days building sand-castles and writing to their pen-pals in France. By this time most people in Britain and the rest of the world had reached middle age. Hence this period in history became known as The Middle Ages.

KNIGHTS

Although daytime in the Middle Ages was rather dull, knights were, in fact, great fun. The only trouble was, if you wanted to be a great knight, you had to have a big kitchen.

TYPICAL KNIGHT IN SHINING ARMOUR

SAUCEPAN

DUSTBIN LID

'DRAIN PIPES'

TIN CANS → SOUP

BEANS

WATER BARREL

BREAD TINS

Knights went to tournaments to practise jousting, which involved putting a tablecloth on a horse and charging up and down with a large broom in your hand. At the end of the jousting contest the knight would ride up to a fair lady who would place her dirty washing on the end of his broom handle. Records tell us that, because knights became extremely cold wearing suits of armour, this custom became known as 'shivery', which was later changed to chivalry. (When knights used brooms it was known as shovelry.)

CHAPTER FOURTEEN:
THE RENAISSANCE

After the Middle Ages there followed a very exciting period in Europe when everyone wanted to learn to do new things. This period was called 'The Renaissance', which is a French word meaning something in French. Here are some of the things they learnt:

PAINTING

Before the Renaissance, people painted extremely strange-looking things, like other people, for instance. During the fifteenth century however, artists began to take their art a lot more seriously and painted new and interesting things, like garage doors, fingernails and the odd gate.

SERIOUS RENAISSANCE ART

Leonardo da Vinci was one of the greatest artists that ever lived. He was also a brilliant mathematician. During the Renaissance Leondardo combined these two skills and invented 'Painting by Numbers' – a technique that has inspired great artists through the centuries.

Here is an unfinished painting by Leonardo. See if you can finish it off by painting by numbers.

1. Brown
2. Light brown
3. Dark brown
4. Even darker brown
5. Brownish
6. Browner

Note: try to make your painting as colourful as possible.

Michael and Gelo also lived at the time of the Renaissance. By night they worked as great artists and by day, as plumbers who were constantly being called in to mend the cistern chapel. It was in fact Michael and Gelo who invented the brilliant technique known today as 'Joining the Dots'. These great artists spent many days lying upside down joining the dots on cathedral ceilings. Here are some unfinished dots by Michael and Gelo. See if you can join them up.

Figurino was the great Renaissance artist who invented the technique of 'Figure Drawing'. Here is Figurino painting his most famous painting of the figure 4. Can you guess what his next painting was?

Painting Nude: For the first time ever, artists began painting 'nude'. Here is a photograph of the famous artist Botticelli painting in the nude.

Perspective: Renaissance artists also learned how to show distance in their paintings. This meant that they could walk inside them when they felt like it. In fact once they were in, many artists decided not to come out at all.

OTHER THINGS LEARNED BY PEOPLE DURING THE RENAISSANCE AGE:–

Car maintenance, Windsurfing, American Football, Rapping, Train spotting, Bopping, hopping, and the electric guitar.

THINGS TO DO

▼

1. Walk into a painting
2. Join up your spots.

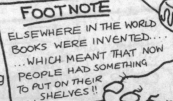

FOOTNOTE
ELSEWHERE IN THE WORLD BOOKS WERE INVENTED....
...WHICH MEANT THAT NOW PEOPLE HAD SOMETHING TO PUT ON THEIR
...SHELVES !!

HENRY THE ⅛th

Henry the ⅛th is most famous for having six wives. This is not true however. Henry had only one wife who simply had six heads.

LADY JANE GREY

Lady Jane Grey was the shortest queen to have ever ruled. She was in fact only one inch tall. Unfortunately Queen Jane had her head cut off only a week and a half after she accepted the job, which made her even shorter.

WILLIAM THE ORANGE

William the Orange, nicknamed 'Pip', was most famous being married to Mary, the **apple** of his eye. Pip was, according to legend, a bit of a **lemon** but did live a long and **fruity** life and he and Mary were indeed a lovely **pear**.

LIZ THE FIRST

Liz the first was one of the greatest queens that ever lived. She was, however, a bit of a pain in the neck which meant that her neck had to be permanently bandaged. Her favourite courtier was a chap named Sir Walter Raleigh, who invented the bike and had a rather strange habit of putting his coat in puddles.

MARY QUEEN OF SPOTS

Mary Queen of Spots unfortunately became so spotty she had to have her head chopped off. Unfortunately it didn't cure her spots.

LOUIS XIV OF FRANCE

Louis XIV of France was most famous for being a long-haired layabout who walked round in skirts all day. Unfortunately Louis XIV took so long to get dressed in the morning – as was the fashion at that time – that by the time he was ready it was time for him to get undressed again. For this reason – Louis was not seen for many years.

69

WILL SHAKESPEARE

Will Shakespeare was the greatest playwright ever to have lived. Below is a sample from perhaps his most famous work, *Romeo and Juliet*. See if you can spot the mistake in this verse.

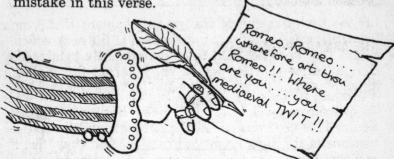

Christopher Columbus, Francis Drake and Walter Raleigh were all famous explorers of this age.

Hidden in the picture below are ten things these explorers took with them on their voyages. Can you spot them? If you can't, draw them in.

1. A ship 2. Suntan lotion 3. Bucket and spade 4. Swimming Trunks 5. Rubber ring 6. Passport 7. Toothbrush 8. Money for postcards 9. A stuffed donkey 10. Camera

THINGS TO DO

▼

- If there is a maritime museum near where you live – push it in and see if it floats!
- Visit a balcony.

THE ARMADA PUZZLE PAGE

In 1588 Phil the First of Spain sent a huge fleet to Plymouth to do battle against England. Its mission was to overthrow Queen Liz and make England Catholic again. This fleet was called the Armada, and the battle was one of the most important battles of all time. See if you can answer the following important questions:–

1. What colour were Phil the First's tights?

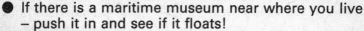

2. Which of these two flags was used by the English fleet?

3. What size hips did Liz the First have?

4. What kind of things could you buy in the Armada Duty Free shop?

5. What kind of vessel did Francis Drake sail around the world in:-

a) A rubber ring   b) A surf board   c) A pedal boat

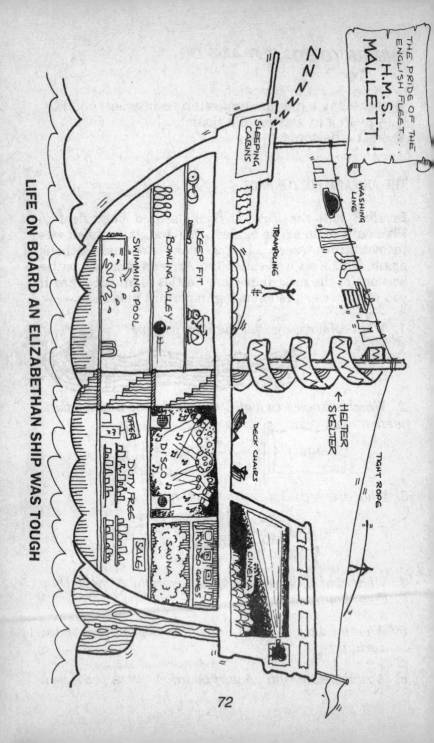

LIFE ON BOARD AN ELIZABETHAN SHIP WAS TOUGH

THE PRIDE OF THE ENGLISH FLEET..... H.M.S. MALLETT!

SLEEPING CABINS

SWIMMING POOL

BOWLING ALLEY

KEEP FIT

DUTY FREE

OFFER

SALE

SAUNA

DISCO

VIDEO GAMES

CINEMA

DECK CHAIRS

← HELTER SKELTER

TRAMPOLINE

WASHING LINE

TIGHT ROPE

THINGS TO FIND OUT AND DO

1. Elizabeth I was extremely vain. She wore lavish clothes and whitened her face with a powder made from egg white and powdered eggshell. Try making your own version of Elizabeth's cosmetic recipe and leave it on your face for a week. Use the following ingredients:

Soup
Wallpaper paste
Cement
Mud
Soot

2. Make a life-size model of Philip and float it in your nearest duck pond.

3. Make your own compass. Here's what to do:–
- Cut out a circle from paper
- Mark it with the points of the compass; North, South, East and West
- Draw an arrow in the middle, pointing to the direction you wish to go
- Stick it to the palm of your hand and start your journey, following your hand at all times.

4. *Learn to tie a reef knot. Here's what to do:*

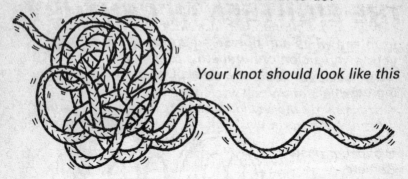

Your knot should look like this

On this piece of paper is a message written by Philip in invisible ink. What is it?

Here is a typical song sung by seamen from the English fleet. Can you finish it off?

CHAPTER SIXTEEN:
THE EIGHTEENTH CENTURY.
AGE OF REVOLUTION

Although people's clothes did improve slightly during the eighteenth century, owing to the discovery of trousers, on the whole times were fairly hard, mainly because the world was plagued by silly and nit-picking little revolutions.

THE AGRICULTURAL REVOLUTION

The Agricultural Revolution was all about agriculture and, so we are told, changed farming methods in Britain for ever, despite the fact that before this people were quite happy to eat frozen peas and carrots and did not care a sprout about what bits of land belonged to who and all that daft organic nonsense.

NEW TOOLS

The Agricultural Revolution led to the invention of new tools to help the farmers plough their land. These new tools were, lawn mowers, electrical hedge trimmers, barbecues, sprinklers, chip slicers and garden gnomes.

NEW CROPS

The Agricultural Revolution also led to the introduction of new crops. As men were at last wearing trousers it seemed natural for them to also get their hair cut. Farmers who did not have crops often found that their long and quite ridiculous curls often got caught up in the mower, causing them to cry.

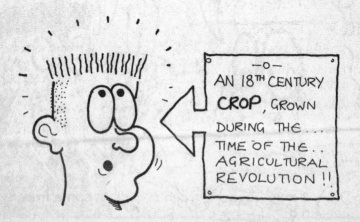

BETTER ANIMALS

During this time farmers also invented newer and better animals to help them produce essential products. These animals were, dinosaurs (see Chapter Two), daddy-long-legs, gerbils, gold fish and mermaids.

Towards the end of the Agricultural Revolution Britain introduced the Corn Laws which made it against the law for anyone to have corns on their feet.

ANCIENT CORN LAW POSTER

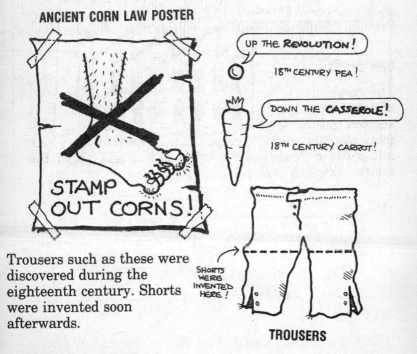

Trousers such as these were discovered during the eighteenth century. Shorts were invented soon afterwards.

TROUSERS

THINGS TO DO

1. Draw a map of your garden and plant some frozen peas in it.

77

THE INDUSTRIAL REVOLUTION

The great Industrial Revolution was even more annoying to those people who lived in the eighteenth century mainly due to the fact that they couldn't walk out of their own front door without bumping into a machine, or being run over by a bus. Here are some of the other changes that came about during this period:

SHOPS

Shops were discovered during the Industrial Revolution. Although this meant that your mum was constantly asking you to pop down the road to get this that and the other every five minutes, it did mean you could take all those awful Christmas presents back and change them for something a lot better.

CLOTH

One of the most interesting inventions invented during the Industrial Revolution was the cloth, which brought with it thousands of machines and factories. The cloth became useful for wiping things up and cleaning windows. This invention was soon followed by the discovery of a cloth used for drying up, known as the Tea Cloth. Other famous cloths were the Face Cloth, the Jay Cloth, the Dish Cloth and the Table Cloth.

STEAM

The invention of steam during the Industrial Revolution meant that at last people could make a decent cup of tea and get their carpets cleaned. Steam also became useful for opening people's letters without them catching on and for clearing your nose when it was blocked up.

SOME STEAM INVENTED DURING THE INDUSTRIAL REVOLUTION

THE FRENCH REVOLUTION AND NAPOLEONIC WARS

Meanwhile in France a few other nasty goings-on were going on.

The French Revolution came about in France when a bunch of french Frenchmen took it upon themselves to execute a lot of people. This they did by asking them to bend down underneath a giant cheese-slicer known as the guillotine, which cut off their heads. A lot of people objected to having their heads cut off in this way and did in fact write to complain about it afterwards.

THE STORY OF NAPOLEON

Before long, a brave and courageous soldier called Napoleon was crowned Emperor of France. He and his wife Not Tonight Josephine were an extremely nice couple and, even though Napoleon had one arm permanently in his pocket, he still managed to decorate the house and play ping pong in his spare time.

Unfortunately for Napoleon, however, he got into a bit of a scrap at Waterloo Station on the way to work one day and has never been seen since.

QUIZ

NAPOLEON'S VICTORIOUS ARMIES.... ..BEFORE THE BATTLE OF PORTALOO !!

1. Napoleon was very famous for wearing a certain kind of hat. Which one of these hats belonged to him?

2. Which famous Duke defeated Napoleon at the Battle of Waterloo?

a. Duke of Plimsole
b. Duke of Slipper
c. Duke of Flip flop
d. Duke of Hush Puppy

Ancient letter of complaint written by a French person who had his head chopped off in the guillotine:

> Dear Sir
>   I would like to complain about my head being chopped off last Tuesday. I did not ask for it to be chopped off and would very much like it back as I am unable to go out of the house. I look forward to you reply
>   Mr Headless

Meanwhile Britain had seen the birth of parliament, which was, at the time, being led by a group of politicians known as the Whigs. Here are some of their famous members:

CURLY TOP

JOHNNY LONGLOCKS

SIR SPIKEY

PETER PLAIT

CHAPTER SEVENTEEN:
THE NINETEENTH CENTURY

*Meanwhile in Britain, the Industrial and Agricultural
Revolutions were still going on, which meant that people
spent most of their days throwing machines and carrots
at each other and generally being very disruptive indeed.*

QUEEN VIC

One of the most famous people involved with the nine-teenth century was indeed our own Queen Vic, who, as it happens, was named after the railway station where she spent much of her youth train-spotting. Queen Vic was crowned Queen of England in 1837, when an extremely clever person spotted her resemblance to the woman on the back of all Victorian coins.

AS VICTORIAN FURNITURE WAS VERY HARD , MOST WOMEN TOOK A SPARE BOTTOM WITH THEM.. ..AT ALL TIMES!..

VICTORIAN FASHION

One of the most important inventions invented during the Industrial Revolution was the mirror. Indeed, many Victorians fainted when they saw what utter clots they had looked during the eighteenth century and decided to spend the rest of their lives smartening up.

THE GROWTH OF TOWNS

The growth of towns was one of the most important developments during Victorian times. In fact towns grew so rapidly that often people went to bed in London and woke up in Scotland.

POOR PEOPLE

Many people were extremely poor during the Victorian age. Here is a typical poor person's daily diet:–

BREAKFAST
One cornflake or one rice Krispie

LUNCH
One teaspoon of soup served with one grain of rice or one green bean

SNACK
One cake crumb or one bit of Kit-kat

DINNER
One smell of Hot Pot served with a picture of roast chicken

OFF TO SCHOOL

After 1870 poor Victorian children were sent to school instead of working in factories. Here they learned the '3 Rs' which were riting, rithmatic and rabbiting on. Unfortunately they did not learn to spell until 6 centuries later.

GREAT WARS THROUGHOUT THE UTTERLY BRILLIANT HISTORY OF THE WORLD . . .

CHAPTER EIGHTEEN:
THE TWENTIETH CENTURY

Surprisingly enough, very little is known about the twentieth century apart from the fact that it is still going on. Nevertheless, perhaps the most devastatingly important event known to twentieth century man was, of course, the birth of me, which took place on a day that shook the earth and rattled the planets. This day will go down in history as the most utterly important day in the Utterly Brilliant History of the World — my birthday.

HOW PEOPLE LIVED IN THE TWENTIETH CENTURY

About 100 years ago, town houses were joined up in rows. These were known as terraced houses. Unfortunately these houses made life very confusing as often people would return to the wrong house. Many families got mixed up during this period in history. Moving house did not solve this problem as many houses were very heavy.

THE AGE OF TECHNOLOGY

During the twentieth century a great revolution took place that changed for ever the way people lived and worked. Many sophisticated gadgets and electrical appliances came over from America to take part in what has become known as 'The Great Technological Revolution'.

FASHION IN THE TWENTIETH CENTURY

Although fashion did improve during this period in history, it also became extremely confusing. Here are some extremely confusing examples:

During the sixties, many women started wearing the mini. This was extremely uncomfortable.

Other women began to wear bee hives on their heads. This was also extremely uncomfortable.

Bell bottoms made creeping up on people very difficult.

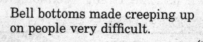

The kipper tie became fashionable but gave rise to the Cod War.

FOOD IN THE TWENTIETH CENTURY

Another important invention invented in America was Fast Food. However, this food was so fast that it had gone by the time it got to people's mouths.

TRANSPORT IN THE TWENTIETH CENTURY

Apart from the invention of the car, the boat, the train, the aeroplane and the foot, one of the most inventive inventions was the rocket, which was great for bonfire night. It also went into space.

HOW TO GET INTO SPACE

Move things out of the way. This creates a space. Step into it.

THINGS TO TAKE INTO SPACE WITH YOU

- *Your autograph book. You will meet many stars.*
- *A duster. Space is full of particles of dust.*
- *A Star Trek video. So you know where to go.*
- *Your trainers. So you can join in the space race.*
- *Your country's flag. In case you forget where you come from.*
- *A spacesuit. In case there's a fancy-dress competition.*
- *A bunch of friends and some party hats. There's never any atmosphere in space.*

TIMMY-LEVEL EXAM

NOW THAT YOU KNOW JUST ABOUT **EVERYTHING** THERE IS TO KNOW ABOUT THE 'UTTERLY BRILLIANT' HISTORY OF THE WORLD, IT'S TIME NOW TO TEST YOUR KNOWLEDGE IN THIS UTTERLY HARD **EXAM!!**

There are certain things that you may take with you into this examination. These are as follows:–

● As many books as you can carry. Cheating is not allowed but you may look the answers up in books.
● A pair of binoculars. These may also come in handy for cheating.
● A skipping rope. If you cannot answer a question – skip on to the next.
● A pen. This is useful in an exam.
● Your brain. You may wish to use it.

TIME ALLOWED: three weeks and ten days.

1. Which of the following Kings was called George?

a) George I
b) George II
c) George III

2. The rulers of ancient Greece found many new colonies. Where were they?

a) Down the back of their wardrobes
b) Buried in the garden
c) Inside Christmas crackers

3. Where did Alexander lead his army?

a) Up his sleevy
b) Up the garden path
c) Up and down

4. What was Napoelon's hand doing inside his jacket?

a) Putting on his deodorant
b) Hiding his dirty nails
c) Looking for his pet hamster

5. Why did the Vikings wear horns?

a) So that they could 'toot' other boats that got in their way
b) Just in case the ice-cream man ran out of cones
c) So they always knew which way up to stand

6. Why was the Great Wall of China so long?

a) They had a big garden
b) They had to use all the bricks up
c) If it was any shorter, it wouldn't be long enough

7. Why was King Richard called Richard 'the Lion Heart'?

a) Because his mum and dad were Mr and Mrs Lion Heart
b) He was an early transplant patient
c) He wasn't

8. **One of the soldiers below is a Roundhead. Can you guess which one?**

9. **What happened at the Boston Tea Party?**

a) *They took the biscuit*
b) *They turned over a new leaf*
c) *They all had jelly and ice-cream*

10. **Which European ruler was known as the 'Sun King'?**

a) *King Norman of Majorca*
b) *Eric the Tanned*
c) *Lady Jane Sandcastle*

11. **What were Caesar's last words before he was murdered by Brutus?**

a) *Hello Brutus!*
b) *That's a nice knife*
c) *Ouchhhhhhh. . . . .*

12. **Why did they say that Rome wasn't built in a day?**

a) *Because it wasn't*
b) *Because they didn't have days in those days*
c) *It's a misprint. They said Rome wasn't built on a tray.*

THE FUTURE

Surprisingly enough we know more about the future than about any other period in history. Here is a picture of everyday life in the future:–